PIECES OF THE PAST

PRISHITA JAISWAL

EDITED BY : RANITHA JOEL

Dedicated to Miss Ranitha

My high school English teacher, who has inspired and motivated me.

To the one who saw the best in me.

Thank you miss

Author's Note

Dear Readers,

Thank you for choosing to dive into these pages. It means the world to me that you're here. This is my first book, a humble beginning, and while it may not yet be flawless, I'm committed to growing as a writer. I hope you find something special within these words, and I'm excited to keep improving, one page at a time.

Being a novice writer, I don't have many poems in my collection. However, this book is a bit of a "salad" (humour, please), with a range of poetry that may complement one another or entirely stand alone. Your interpretation of these poems is purely based on your imagination, experiences, inventiveness, and comprehension skills.

As you journey through these poems, I encourage you to see beyond the words. While some pieces stem from the bonds of friendship, don't hesitate to interpret them through the lens of romantic love if that's what resonates with you. My intention is for these poems, born from my own life and moments of inspiration, to be versatile and reflective of your experiences as well. I hope you find a piece of yourself within these lines and enjoy reading this book as much as I enjoyed creating it.

Thank you.

Acknowledgement

My deepest gratitude belongs to my English teacher, Miss Ranitha Joel. What began as a spontaneous outlet — scribbling poetry whenever inspiration struck or emotions overflowed—grew into something far more meaningful under her guidance. While I provided the words, it was she who truly unlocked my potential. She encouraged, mentored, and tirelessly honed my writing, from my proudest works to my most challenging pieces.

Her unwavering support transformed my casual interest in English into a deep, abiding love for the craft. Every step of my journey as a writer is a testament to her dedication and belief in my abilities, and for that, I am profoundly grateful.

I also wish to express my heartfelt gratitude to Sir Shelby Stephen, a truly inspirational figure who pushed me to strive even harder. His words resonated deeply, stirring my soul and fuelling my determination. From offering insightful suggestions to guiding me through the publishing process, he has been a steadfast support at every step.

Both of these remarkable teachers have been my mentors and guiding lights, my North stars on this journey. To anyone who doubts the existence of extraordinary teachers, I urge you to think again. It took each of them less than ten minutes to inspire me immensely from our very first encounter.

I want to extend my thanks to my publishers, Notion Press, for bringing my dream to life in the most beautiful way possible.

I'm also deeply grateful to my parents, friends, the nature, and the countless random objects, strangers, and fleeting moments that sparked my inspiration.

And to you, my dear readers, I'm endlessly thankful. Your decision to pick up this book means the world to me. Thank you, thank you all, for joining me on this journey!!!

Contents

Something So Beautiful
Part I

To let go of something so beautiful

Is like,

To not discover the vastness of the undiscovered sky

To not explore the depth of the unexplored ocean.

To let go of something so beautiful

Is like,

To not know what lies in the depth of one's eye,

To let go of something so beautiful

Is a pity.

Something So Beautiful
Part II

To see something so beautiful

Fall apart,

Slowly but not steadily.

To see something so treasured

Slip past your fingers,

Like water.

Something that was such a beauty

Now a disaster,

Like never before

What has this friendship become?

I can only ask

But never answer.

1:30 am

Dark, ink-like, pitch black.

With silence,

Sparkling with bespangling stars,

Dancing throughout until dawn.

A gleaming lunette

Illuminating the Earth,

Gazing down,

With the quiet company of the stars.

Only the nocturnals know

Of such ethereal beauty,

In the eerie darkness

That the night sky beholds.

This is the empty darkness,

That fills the lacuna

In the heart of nyctophiles.

This orphic, untamed beauty

Holds the whelving secrets

Of those who live, unlike others,

Not during the day, but at night.

Dead

To be dead and gone

To lie cold and bloodless

As the crimson flowed out of me

Slow but steadily

But also, rapidly.

I knew I had found peace

Solitude, somewhere

I knew a burden had been reduced

From the lives of many

So please.

Let me go

Hate me,

Erase me,

Destroy me,

Whatever is left of me

Let it go.

An Ode to 'Them'

When you thought once someone,

Would be your forever

But only turned out to be

A never-ending heartache,

A bittersweet mistake,

A lifelong regret.

All those promises u made,

All of them fake.

Now I only stare upon

What's left of us.

You said you loved me

But did you really?

As the wind blows,

The echoes of love, fade

So fast,

One can barely think

What and when

It all happened.

So let the wind of change,

Blow the sorrow away.

And let the gentle breeze,

Bring happiness.

Learning from the past

And embracing the newfound present.

A once believing forever,

Now all in the past.

As life plays its symphony

This too shall pass.

In the tapestry of time

A new dream, shall be rediscovered.

The Night

In the solitude of the night,

Where our laughter echoed

And our shadows flowed

Through the streets that we roamed.

An unbreakable pair we were,

Those moments now gone.

Left in despair

Your heart seemingly bare

Seems like you don't care.

I miss the way we'd light up the sky

And conquer the night

The way we'd defy imperfections,

The magic of our connections

Now, I just wonder where it all went wrong.

All those memories,

Those wondrous sights

Thought we'd watch sunsets

See the stars align

But now, your rage is all that's mine.

Now, I sit here all alone beneath the same sky,

And ponder, was it my carelessness

That led to this ?

All those places,

Memories now fade.

Was it all fake?

Those promises made,

Filled with agony and pain

Forever gone now, a friendship now worn

Just a heart left torn.

Beneath the Stars

I sit here beneath the stars

Relive our memories from the past

Like nothing had ever changed

Like it was all the same again.

But now it all seems so far,

I laugh at all the things from the past

Cause' I guess it was all the last

All our memories now in the past

Where the echoes of our laughter were heard

Now silence is all that reigns

A walk down memory lane

Now such a pain.

No more spontaneous texts

Of random things we did

Of silly little GIFs

Just silence.

I listen to the recording on my phone

Your voice on replay as you sing

The sound of your keyboard

Every chord you play.

A crack,
And then silence

As the audio ended

Just like our friendship did.

Promises

All our promises

Shattered now,

Shattered to shards

Like glass.

Scattered on the floor

Left like an open door.

Secrets unfold

Those lies we told.

Now, I stand here and watch

As the light reflects upon each shard

A reflection of our past

A beautiful tapestry of lies.

Broken Tunes

Your voice once soothing

Now I shudder at the sound of it

Our memories a haze,

Now I fear even meeting your gaze.

The time we'd spent

I'd look back at with content.

Now each thought runs a shiver down my spine

In fear of breaking something so divine.

We'd made a bond so strong

No force was able to bend.

Now it's a walk on fragile glass,

One wrong step and it'll all end.

The rhythm of the song we played

Now gone.

The melody we sang,

Now cacophony.

Each word unspoken

A fragile thread,

I fear to speak

My heart fills with dread.

Every glance you give,

Every sigh you heave,

Feels like

A bridge about to break.

Your eyes once warm

Now icy cold,

Used to brim with tender care

Now burn with hostile, angry glare.

I sit here beneath the cold distant moon

And play our broken tune.

Fearing,

Maybe, this is how you wanted this to end?

Although hoping,

That you'll let me in someday,

To fix this mess

To start again.

Why?

Why'd you act like you care?

Say all those words you never meant

Why'd you hold me tight?

When you planned to leave at night.

Why'd you make all those promises?

Make me feel alright?

When you weren't gonna stay afterall

If you were gonna leave at nightfall.

Nights once spent on calls,

Now I falter between love and disdain,

For all the things you did, all the time spent,

Those messages sent.

How much of that was truly you?

Did any of it matter to you?

Did I ever,

Mean anything to you?

People

We're all a mosaic of people

A little bit of this,

A little bit of that.

A bit of every person

We've ever met in our lives,

Left a little bit of them inside us.

Enemy, lover, friend or family

A bit of them all

Has made a lot of us.

Scars of the Sun

I knew caring for you

Meant reaching for the sun,

Whose flames would burn me through

Turn me to ash

And leave me lost, out of view.

Yet I loved you,

Not as your lover

But as your friend, for all I knew

I never really did believe-

In love so romantic that it's true.

So blinded by the rays of the sun

I cared for you,

I played with fire for fun.

Burned my hands

Just so I could feel the warmth of one.

I cared,

So much

So that, no more I cared

If the sun's flames turned me to ash,

Burned me bare.

And anyways, they would tell

"Love is blind",

And deep in your eyes, blindly, I fell,

Hazel they would shine

As the rays hit well.

"Death leaves a heartache no one can heal,

And love,

Leaves memories no one can steal"

And so the end of this love's appeal

Left me with scars that won't fade,

For out of all the wounds that refuse to heal,

Yours is the one that bleeds

For your love left a void no time can repeal.

Goodbye/Strangers With Memories [1]

I had a dream last night,

It was one of those nightmares.

I wanted to call you, text you

Tell you about it

You'd ease the storm within

Whisper that it's okay.

---

[1] Dear readers, this is your author just here to let you all know that this poem has two titles separated by the "/". Given my indecisive nature I decided to give the poem two titles.

But then reality struck,

We're no longer the friends we used to be.

Now we're, as they say,

"Strangers with memories."

Even though I see you

Every single day.

I no longer have the courage,

To speak to you.

I fear the sound of my favourite tunes

Each one evokes me of you

And when each song pipes into my head

I hear not the singer

But your utter

As you'd reembody it on your keyboard.

I sit on my bench at school

Where once you sat beside me.

Caught in a cascade of our reminiscence

Now it runs dry, as each memory flows by.

Today

I had to say goodbye.

Thorns of Love

Every rose has its thorn,

Touch it and you'll be forlorn,

Your flesh shall be torn,

Blood shall pour like a storm,

A reminder of love's scorn.

Blinded so much by adoration,

You forget your own salvation,

Lost in the fragrant temptation,

Till pain becomes your revelation,

A truth that cuts with cold precision.

Once a seed now a flower

Beauty is in the eye of the beholder

Beauty is the pain that must shudder,

The one that waters

Knows, for flower to grow, bud must falter.

Silent storms sweep the sky,

Neither hear each other's cry

Bitter beauty must rely

On the tears that time can't dry

For wounds that linger never lie.

Time may be ceased,

But wounds will be creased,

Hearts may be leased,

But once broken will bleed.

Photograph

We keep this love in a photograph

Corners thinned, frayed and worn

Like the vows we swore in our youths laugh

To stay by each other's side even if time
turned scorn.

The faded smile

Colours gone dim

Memories of erstwhile

Emotions fill to the brim

These paper dreams,

Eyes flickering of mischief

From the old-time schemes

And hearts at peace with bliss.

Worlds we feared to be forgotten

Captured in sections, preserved till the end

Now a museum of paper, time-begotten

Fragments of history that forever transcend

Laugh at our cries,

Oh, the irony of life and its past,

Cry at our laughs

The memories of life now forever in our cast.

Over You

Thought I was over you

Thought I finally let it all go,

Thought I wouldn't care, for all my might

And then, you showed up in my dream last night.

Read your text with pain

Your reply filled with disdain

Yet in my dream

It wasn't all so extreme...

-

All these poems unwritten

Maybe someday I'll find the vision,

To fill the gaps that I've been given,

With words that I want written.

Hearts breaks I used to fear

But these broken ties now severe

Friendships I thought would be aged

But now they're left decayed.

I believed in amity

But found love not so witty

Was it my fault?

Should I have let my beliefs halt?

Or was it that I believed,

When I never should have conceived?

But isn't this also heartbreak and heartache,

Even if it's not a romantic mistake?

This one is where I believed persistently,

The one where I trusted earnestly.

Because

It was a bond for a cause.

This one is where I gave it my all

Sacrificed my call

Because,

It was a bond for a cause.

The one where I didn't care,

For anything or anywhere.

Because it wasn't love to spare,

Just a feeling that wasn't there.

But I was mistaken,

Wrong this entire time, forsaken

Hearts were taken

Love was shaken, trust was broken.

Lent you my heart

Right from the start

Should've known you'd set it apart

Left with fragments, this wretched work of art.

An epiphany struck, I thought I was done,

But still, I'm not over you, the pain's not gone,

Each memory lingers, like a battle lost and won,

I thought I was over it, but it's just begun.

I wonder, if you ever think of me,

Recall the things we used to be,

If your best songs remind you of me

If you still care for me.

Each memory set on replay

Something I can't let get away,

Like the songs I'm enthralled to play

Where every note echoes the pain, you left to stay.

Unfinished, with words left untold,

A flood of thoughts, both timid and bold,

Some days they flow, but others, I'm cold,

Too numb to write, my story unfolds.